Excel 2016 Basics

A Quick And Easy Guide To Boosting Your Productivity With Excel

NATHAN GEORGE

ISBN: 1546980172
ISBN-13: 978-1546980179

The information given in this book is given in good faith and belief in its accuracy at the time of publication. The author and publishers disclaim any liability arising directly or indirectly from the use, or misuse, of the information contained in this book.

CONTENTS

INTRODUCTION

Excel 2016 Basics covers all you would need to successfully create workbooks with Excel to provide solutions for your data. You learn how to create, edit, format, and print your worksheets. The book also covers the most popular functions in Excel as well as creating tables and different types of charts.

This book is concise and to the point as you don't need to wade through a wall of text to learn how to quickly carry out a task in Excel. Hence you will not see the unnecessary verbosity and filler text you may find in some other Excel books in this book. The aim is to take even a complete beginner to someone that is skilled in Excel within a few short hours.

Who Is This Book For?

Excel 2016 Basics is suitable for someone who is new to Excel or spreadsheets in general, or someone with intermediate Excel skills intending to learn some of the new features in Excel 2016. If you are already very good with Excel and seeking to learn some of the more advanced topics like Pivot Tables, What-If Analysis, Macros etc. then this book is not for you.

This book is aimed at readers with Microsoft Excel 2016, however, many of the core Excel features remain the same for earlier versions of Excel, like Excel 2010 and Excel 2013. So, you would still find many of the lessons in this book relevant even if you have an earlier version of Excel.

As much as possible, I point out the features new in Excel 2016 when covered. Note however that if you're using an earlier version of Excel, many of the file related tasks described in this book may not match your old version of Excel. This is due to Microsoft changing command options and the screens for many file-related tasks.

How To Use This Book

This book can be used as a step-by-step training guide as well as a reference manual that you come back to from time to time. You can read it cover to cover or skip to certain parts that cover topics you want to learn. Although the chapters have been organised in a logical manner, the book has been designed to enable you to read a chapter as a standalone tutorial to learn how to carry out a certain task.

There are many ways to carry out the same task in Excel, so, for brevity, I have focused on the most efficient way of carrying out a task. On some occasions, however, I also provided alternative ways to carry out a task.

As much as possible, the menu items and commands mentioned are bolded to distinguish them from the other text. I have also included many images to illustrate the features and tasks being discussed.

Assumptions

The software and hardware assumptions made when writing this book is that you already have Excel 2016 installed on your computer and that you're working on the Windows 7, 8 or 10 platforms. If you are using Excel 2016 on a Mac, then simply substitute any Windows keyboard commands mentioned in the book for the Mac equivalent. All the features within Excel remain the same for both platforms.

If you're using Excel on a tablet or touchscreen device, again, simply substitute any keyboard commands mentioned in the book with the equivalent on your touchscreen device.

1 GETTING STARTED WITH EXCEL

Click on the Windows start menu and scroll down to the group of applications starting with E. You'll see Excel as part of the list.

To be able to access Excel faster next time you can pin it to the **Start menu, Taskbar**, or place a shortcut on your **desktop**.

To pin Excel to your Start menu:

1. Click on the Windows **Start menu**.
2. Scroll down to the group of applications under **E**.
3. Right-click **Excel 2016** and select **Pin to Start**.

To pin Excel to your Taskbar:

1. Click on the **Start menu**.
2. Scroll down to the group of applications under **E**.
3. Right-click **Excel 2016** and select **More > Pin to taskbar**.

To place a copy of Excel's shortcut on your desktop:

1. Click on the **Start menu**.
2. Right-click on Excel 2016 and select **More > Open file location**.

This will open the shortcut folder location of Excel 2016.

3. In the folder, right-click on Excel 2016 and click on **Copy**.
4. On your desktop, right-click any area and select **Paste**.

Creating A New Excel Workbook

Launch Excel from the start menu or the icon you have created on your taskbar or desktop.

Excel will launch to the start screen. The Excel 2016 start screen enables you to create a new blank workbook or open one of your recently opened workbooks. You also have predefined templates on the start screen that you can use as the basis of your workbook.

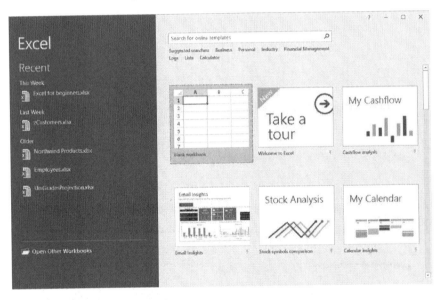

To create a new workbook, click on **Blank workbook**. This will create a new workbook with a worksheet named **Sheet1**.

Another way to quickly create a new workbook when you already have a workbook open is to type **CTRL + N** on your keyboard. This will create a new workbook named **Book1**.

Saving Your Excel Workbook

To save your workbook:

1. Click on the disk icon on the top-left of the window, or click on **File > Save As**.
2. On the next screen, click on **OneDrive – Personal** (if you're using OneDrive) or **This PC** (if you're not saving it to OneDrive).
3. On the right side of the page, you get a text box to enter the file name. Enter the name of your worksheet here.
4. If you want to save it to a folder/sub-folder, navigate to the folder by double-clicking on the folder.
5. Click on the **Save** button to save the workbook.

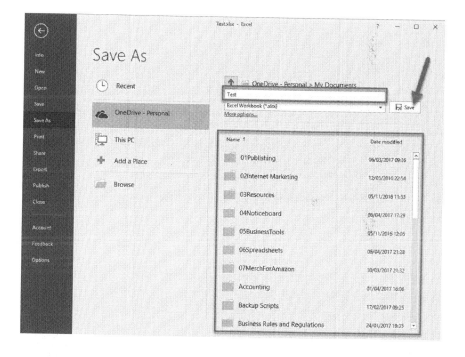

You'll be taken back to the **Home** tab after the file has been saved.

The Excel User Interface

In this chapter, I'll briefly cover the Excel 2016 user interface so you're familiar with the names for various parts of the interface I'll be mentioning throughout the book.

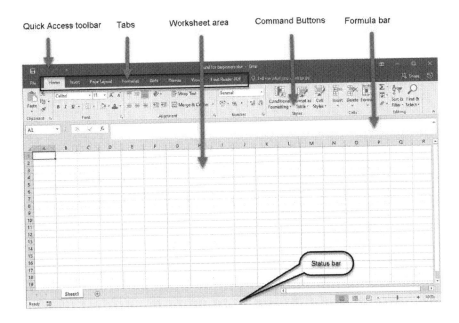

The **File** menu item when clicked opens a window with several menu options, including **Info**, **New**, **Open**, **Save**, **Save As**, **Print**, **Share**, **Export**, and **Close**. At the bottom of the list, you have the **Account** menu option where you view your user information. You also have **Options** where you can change many of Excel's default settings.

To exit the File screen and go back to your worksheet, click on the back button (the left-pointing arrow at the top-left of the page).

The **Quick Access Toolbar** is an area where you can add commands that you can quickly access, hence the name. To add commands to the quick access bar, click on the drop-down arrow to get a drop-down list, then check the command you want to add by selecting it.

The tabs in Excel provide different sets of command buttons geared to different tasks.

The **Home** tab provides the most used set of commands. The other tabs provide command buttons for specific tasks like inserting objects into your spreadsheet, formatting the page layout, working with formulas, working with datasets, reviewing your spreadsheet etc.

The worksheet area contains the cells that will hold your data. The row headings are numbered while the columns heading have letters. Each cell is identified by the combination of the column letter and row number. So, for example, the first cell on the on the sheet is A1, the second cell in the first row is B1 and the second cell in the first column is A2. You use these references to identify the cells on the worksheet.

A **workbook** is the Excel document itself. A **worksheet** is a sheet inside a workbook. Each workbook can have several worksheets. You can use the tabs at the bottom of the screen to add, name, move, copy, and delete worksheets.

The **Formula bar** displays the contents of the active cell including any formula.

The **Status bar** provides information on the current display mode and allows you to zoom in and out of your spreadsheet by clicking on the + and - signs at the bottom-right of the screen.

The **Dialogue Box** launcher is a diagonal arrow in the lower-right corner of some groups. When clicked it opens a window containing additional task options related to that group. So, if you cannot see a command on the Ribbon for a task you want to carry out, click on the small dialogue box launcher to display more options for that group.

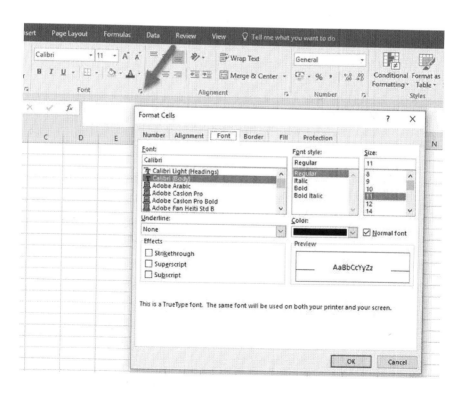

Customising The Ribbon

The area of the screen containing the tabs and command buttons is called the **ribbon**. You can customise the ribbon to your liking by adding or removing tabs and command buttons.

To customise the ribbon, right click anywhere on the ribbon, below the tabs, and select **Customize the Ribbon...** from the pop-up menu.

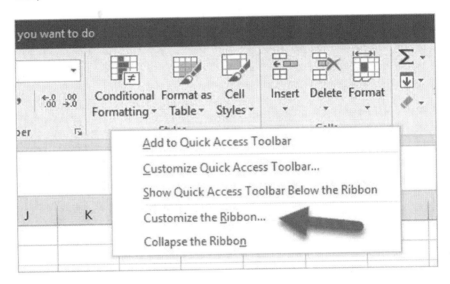

This will open the **Excel Options** window.

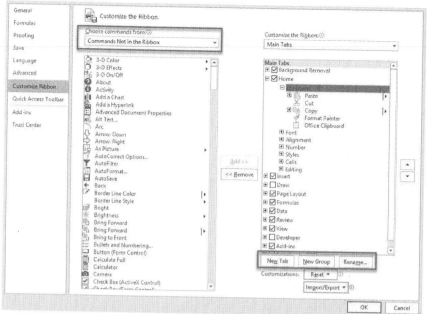

In the **Excel Options** window, the **Customize Ribbon** page will be selected and on that page, you have two main boxes. On the right, you have the box that shows your current tabs - **Main Tabs**. On the left, you have the command buttons that you can add to the ribbon.

To expand a group in the **Main Tabs** box, click on the plus sign (+) on the right of an item. To collapse a group, click on the minus sign (-) on the right of the item.

To find commands that are not currently on your ribbon, click the down arrow on the left box (named **Choose commands from)** and select **Commands Not in the Ribbon** from the drop-down list.

You will see a list of commands that are not on your ribbon. This is useful as it filters out the commands that are already on your ribbon.

Note: You cannot add or remove the default commands on the ribbon but you can uncheck them on the list to prevent them from being displayed. Also, you cannot add command buttons to the default groups. You must create a new group to add a new command button.

To create a new tab:

Click on the **New Tab** button to create a new tab. Within the tab, you must create at least one group before you can add a command button from the left side of the screen.

To create a custom group:

Select the tab in which you want to create the group. This could be one the default tabs or the new one you've created. Click on the **New Group** button (located at the bottom of the screen, under the Main Tabs box). This will create a new group within the currently selected tab. Select the new group and click on **Rename** to give the group your preferred name. You now have a custom group in which you can add commands.

To add commands to your custom group:

Select your custom group in the list on the right side of the screen. Select the new command button you want to add from the list on the left side of the screen. Click on the **Add >>** button to add the command to the new custom group. **Note:** If you want to remove a command from your custom group, select the command on the right box and click **<< Remove**. Click on **OK** to confirm the change. When you view the customised tab on the ribbon you'll see your new group and the command buttons you've added.

Accessing Help In Excel

To access **Help** in Excel, ensure your workbook is the active window on your desktop, then press **F1** on your keyboard. This will open the Help pane on the right side of the screen and you can search for the topic you want help on.

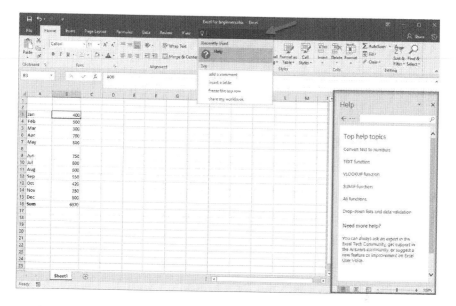

Another quick way to display the **Help** pane is to simply type in "help" in the **Tell Me** search box. The first item on the list will display the Help pane when clicked.

The **Tell Me** help feature (Alt+Q) is a new feature starting with Excel 2016. It will list the command sequence for the help topic you've entered and even help you in completing the command sequence by taking you to the appropriate screen. You can access this feature in the **Tell me what you want to do** box on the ribbon.

When you click on **Tell me what you want to do**, a search box is displayed. Enter a search term to display a drop-down list of options related to your search. When you click on an option on the list you'll automatically be taken to the appropriate tab or screen where the task can be carried out. If there is no related screen, then the help pane will be displayed with information related to your search term.

2 DESIGN WORKBOOKS

When you first create a workbook, you'll have one worksheet called **Sheet1**.

To add a new sheet to your workbook, click on the plus sign (+) at the bottom of the worksheet area, to the right of Sheet1 and it will create a new worksheet named Sheet2. You can add more worksheets to your workbook this way.

The number of worksheets you can have in a workbook is unlimited. You're only limited by your computer resources like RAM and hard disk space. However, try not to have too many sheets in one workbook as the file can become very large, taking longer to open.

Naming A Worksheet

To name your worksheet, double-click on the name tab at the bottom of the screen and the name will become editable. For example, if you double-click on *Sheet1* the name will be selected with the cursor blinking, allowing you to type in the new name.

Moving And Copying Your Worksheet

You can move and reorder your worksheets by clicking on the name and dragging it to the left or right. You can also move a sheet by right-clicking on the name and selecting **Move or Copy** from the pop-up menu.

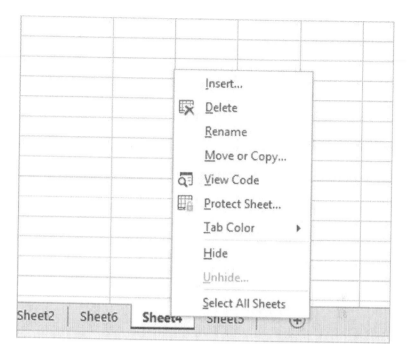

On the **Move or Copy** screen, select a name from the list and click OK. The selected worksheet will be moved to the front of the sheet selected.

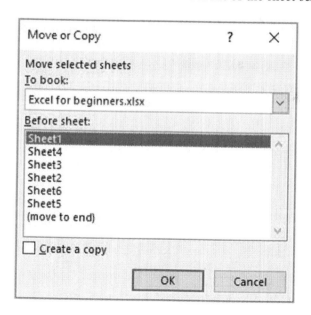

If you want it copied instead of moved, click on the **Create a copy**

check box before clicking OK. A copy will be placed in front of the selected sheet.

Removing A Worksheet

On the Sheet tab, right-click the sheet you want to remove and click **Delete**.

If the sheet is empty, it will be deleted right away. If the sheet has data, then you'll get a pop-up message asking you to confirm the deletion. Click on **Delete** to confirm the deletion.

Hide A Worksheet

On the Sheet tab, right-click the sheet you want to hide and select **Hide**.

To unhide a sheet right-click on any of the Sheet tabs. If a sheet is hidden then the **Unhide** option will be available on the pop-up menu. Select **Unhide** to display a window listing the hidden sheets. You can select any sheet on the list and click **OK** to display it again.

Freezing Rows And Columns

When you have a large worksheet with lots of data, you may want your data headers (row and/or column) to remain visible as you scroll down or to the right of the page.

To make your column headings always visible you can freeze then on the page so that the scroll action does not take them out of view.

To quickly freeze the top row of your worksheet:

1. Click on the **View** tab on the ribbon.
2. In the Window group on the tab, click on **Freeze Panes**.
3. Select **Freeze Top Row**.

When you now scroll down the page the top row will always remain visible.

To quickly freeze the first column of your worksheet:

1. Click on the **View** tab on the ribbon.

2. In the Window group on the tab, click on **Freeze Panes.**
3. Select **Freeze First Column.**

When you now scroll to the right of the page the first column will always remain visible.

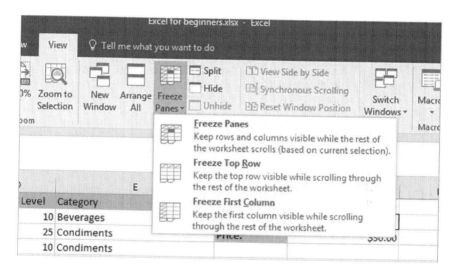

On some occasions, you may want to freeze rows and columns other than the first ones.

To freeze any row of your choosing:

1. Select a cell that is directly under the row you want to freeze to make it the active cell.
2. Click on the **View** tab.
3. In the Window group click on **Freeze Panes.**
4. Select **Freeze Panes** from the pop-up list.

To freeze any column of your choosing:

1. Select a cell on the first row of the column that is to the right of the one you want to freeze. For example, if you want to freeze *column B* then you would select cell *C1*.
2. Click on the **View** tab.
3. In the Window group click on **Freeze Panes.**
4. Select **Freeze Panes** from the pop-up list.

Other examples:

- If you want to freeze the first row and first column of your worksheet, you would select cell **B2** and then select **View > Freeze Panes > Freeze Panes**.
- If you want to freeze only rows 1 and 2, you would select cell **A3** and select **View > Freeze Panes > Freeze Panes**.
- If you want to freeze only columns A and B, you would click on cell **C1** and select **View > Freeze Panes > Freeze Panes**.

To unfreeze any frozen row or columns, click on Freeze Panes and select **Unfreeze Panes** from the pop-up menu.

Applying Themes To Your Worksheet

A theme is a formatting package that you can apply to your worksheet that may include colours for headers, text fonts, the size of cells etc.

There are several themes in Excel that you can apply to your whole worksheet.

To change the look and feel of your worksheet with themes:

1. Click on the **Page Layout** tab on the Ribbon.
2. Click on the **Themes** button to display the drop-down list with many themes you can apply to your worksheet.
3. You can move your mouse pointer over a theme to get a preview of how your worksheet would look with that theme.
4. When you find one that you're happy with, click on it to have it applied to your worksheet.

If you apply a theme you don't like, simply click on the **Undo** button on the Quick Access menu (the left arrow) to undo the changes and return your worksheet back to its previous state.

3 ENTERING AND EDITING DATA

To enter data in Excel, click on a cell in the worksheet area and type in the data. You can change the position of the active cell by using your mouse pointer to point and click on the cell or use your arrow keys to move left, right, up or down.

When typing data in a cell, if you make a mistake use the BACKSPACE key to go back, not your left arrow. The arrows on the keyboard move the cursor from cell to cell.

To overwrite data, click on the cell with the data you want to overwrite and type in the new value. If you do not want to overwrite data but instead you want to edit it, click on the cell and then click in the formula bar to edit the data.

To delete data from your worksheet, select the data and hit the delete key.

In Excel, numbers and formulas are right-aligned in the cell. Everything else is left-aligned. So, you can tell if Excel recognises your entry as a number or text value.

 ## Using AutoFill

The Autofill feature in Excel enables you to fill cells with a series of sequential dates and numbers. It enables you to automate repetitive tasks as it is smart enough to figure out what data goes in a cell, based on another cell, when you drag the fill handle across cells.

Entering Dates With AutoFill

You may have a worksheet where you need to enter dates. You can enter *January* in one cell and used the AutoFill feature to automatically enter the rest of the months.

The **AutoFill handle** is the small + that appears when you move your mouse pointer over the lower right corner of the active cell. So, you first need to click on the cell to select it and then move your mouse pointer over the bottom right corner to display the small plus sign (+).

To AutoFill dates, enter *January* or any other starting month in one cell then grab the small fill handle and drag it across the other cells.

AutoFill also works with abbreviations but they must be 3 letters. For example, if you enter Jan and then drag down, it will be filled with Feb, Mar, Apr, May etc.

Let's say you want to enter the 7 days of the week as your row headings. In the first cell of your range, enter *Monday* or *Mon*. Then drag the autofill handle down over the remaining 6 cells. This will AutoFill the remaining cells with Tuesday to Sunday.

Excel keeps the filled days selected, giving you a chance to drag the handle back if you went too far, or to drag it further if you didn't go far enough.

You can also use the **AutoFill options** drop-down menu to further refine your fill options. To access the AutoFill options, with the cells still selected, you will see a drop-down button that appears on the last cell. When you click on it, you will get a list of options that enable you to select whether you want to copy the data across the cells, fill the series, copy formatting only, ignore the formatting, flash fill etc.

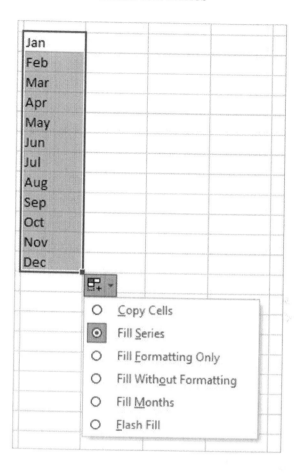

AutoFill Incremental Values

To AutoFill other incremental values, you need to let Excel know what the difference is. So, you would need to enter values in at least two cells before dragging the fill handle across the other cells.

Let's say you want to enter dates that increment by seven days i.e. a weekly interval, you would need to enter two dates (for example, 01/10/17 and 01/17/17). Then you select both cells and drag across the other cells to autofill the other cells with dates having an interval of 7 days.

You can do the same with other numbers. If you enter 1 and then drag down, the number 1 will just be copied to the other cells. However, if you enter numbers 1 and 2 in two cells, and then select them and drag across, you will get 3, 4, 5, 6 etc.

AutoFill Formulas

To AutoFill a formula across several cells enter the formula in the first cell and then drag the fill handle over the other cells in the range. The cell references will also change to match the position of the active cell.

For example, if the first cell of your formula is $= A1 + B1$, when you drag this down to the other cells, the formula in the other cells will be, $=A2+B2$, $=A3+B3$, $=A4+B4$ and so on.

Another way to use AutoFill is to click on the **Fill** button in the **Editing** group on the **Home** tab.

AutoFill The Same Values

To AutoFill the same value across a series of cells, enter the value in the first cell then hold down the CTRL key while dragging the fill handle across the other cells.

For example, if you want to fill a range of cells with $6.99:

1. Enter $6.99 in the first cell.
2. Hold down the CTRL key.
3. Move your mouse pointer to the bottom-right of the cell and grab the fill handle (plus sign) and then drag it across the other cells.

Using Flash Fill

Flash Fill is a new feature in Excel 2016 that enables you to split and combine data automatically.

For example, if you have a name field (made up of the *first name* and *surname*) that you would like to sort by surname. You would need to re-enter the names in another column with the surname first. This is because Excel starts its sorting with the first character of the field, and then the next, and so on.

With Flash Fill, you can insert a new column next to the name column and enter the first value with the surname first. When you enter the second value, Excel will figure out what you're trying to do and automatically Flash Fill the other cells in the format it predicts you want to enter the data. This will save you a lot of time as you only need to enter two cells to have the rest automatically completed for you.

Clipboard	Font			Alignment

B4   ✕ ✓ *fx*   West, Peter

	A	B	C	D	E	F
1						
2			Month 1	Month 2		
3	Jane Smith	Smith, Jane	$1,000.00	$1,100.00		
4	Peter West	West, Peter	$2,000.00	$1,500.00		
5	Derek Brown	Brown, Derek	$1,000.00	$1,200.00		
6	Jason Fields	Fields, Jason	$1,100.00	$1,300.00		
7	Mark Powell	Powell, Mark	$1,500.00	$1,600.00		
8	Julie Rush	Rush, Julie	$1,200.00	$1,300.00		
9						
10						

Steps in Flash Fill:

1. Enter the value in the first cell in the new format.
2. Start entering the second value in the next cell.
3. You'll see a preview of the rest of the column completed with the suggested entries.
4. Press enter to accept the suggestions

Another way to use Flash Fill is to select **Data > Flash Fill** from the ribbon. The **Flash Fill** command button is in the **Data Tools** group on the **Data** tab.

Insert another column to the right of the one with the original data. Then enter the first value and click on the **Flash Fill** command button. This will automatically enter the rest of the data in the corresponding cells in the same format it was entered in the first cell.

4 COPYING AND MOVING DATA

In this chapter, we'll cover how to copy and move data around your worksheet and how to insert rows and columns.

To select a group of cells in Excel:

1. Click on the first cell of the area.
2. Ensure your mouse pointer is a white plus sign
3. Click and drag over the other cells in the range you want to include in the selection.

Copy Data

To copy data:

1. Select the range that you want to copy.
2. On the **Home** tab, click on **Copy** (this is the double paper icon next to the Paste command).
3. You will see a dotted line around the area. This is called the marquee.
4. Click on the first cell of the area where you want to paste the contents.
5. Click on **Paste**.
6. The marquee remains active to let you know that you can carry on pasting the copied content if you wish to paste it in multiple areas. To get rid of the marquee, hit the **ESC** key.

Using Paste Options with copying:

1. On the toolbar, click the **Paste** drop-down button to display a pop-up menu with several pasting options.
2. You can move your mouse pointer over the options to see what each one does. You also see a preview of the paste action on your worksheet.
3. For example, if you want to paste the contents and the column width, you would select the option that says **Keep Source Width (W)**. This is on the second row on the menu.
4. Click on it and the data, formatting and column width will be copied across.
5. Once done, remove the dotted moving line by hitting the ESC key. This tells Excel that you're done with the copying.

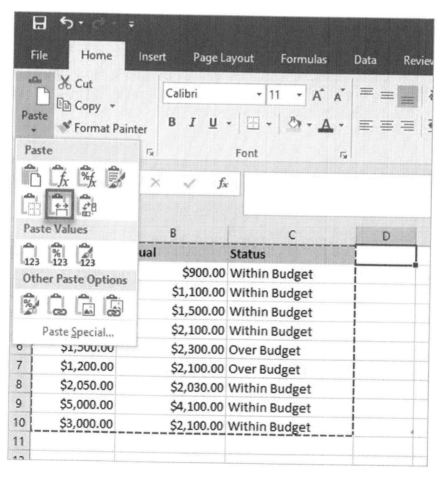

Move Data

To move content, you follow a similar set of actions as we did with copying however, you would **Cut** the data instead of **Copy** it.

1. Select the range you want to move.
2. On the Home tab, click on the **Cut** button (this is the command with the scissors icon).
3. A dotted moving line will appear around the area you've chosen to cut.
4. Place your cursor on the first cell of the area where you want to paste the content. You only need to select one cell.
5. Click on **Paste** on your toolbar. This will move the content from its current location and place it in the area you've chosen.
6. The cut and paste action automatically copies the format of the cells across but not the width. So, you need to adjust the width of the cells if necessary.

Insert Or Delete Rows And Columns

To insert a new column:

Click on the column letter to select the whole column. On the **Home** tab, click on the **Insert** button in the **Cells** group. This will insert a new column to the left of the one you selected. Whenever you need to insert a new column, ensure you select the column immediately to the right of the area where you want to insert a new column.

For example, let's say you have data in columns A, B and C and you wish to insert a new column between A and B. You would select column B and then select **Home** > **Insert** to insert a new column between A and B. The new column will now be the new B.

Inserting a new column by using the pop-up menu:

1. Click the column letter to the right of the insertion point to select the whole column.
2. Right-click and select **Insert** from the pop-up menu. This will insert the new column.

Inserting a new row by using the pop-up menu:

1. Click on the row number directly below the insertion point to select the whole row.
2. Right-click and select **Insert** from the pop-up menu. This will insert a new row directly above the selected row.

You could also insert new rows and columns by using the **Insert** command button on the **Home** tab.

Inserting multiple rows or columns:

1. Hold down the CTRL key.
2. One by one, select the rows up to the number you want to insert. For example, if you want to insert 4 rows then select 4 rows directly under the insertion point.
3. Click on **Home** > **Insert** (or right-click and select **Insert**).

This will insert 4 new rows above the insertion point.

5 FORMATTING CELLS

Resizing Rows And Columns

You can resize rows and columns with your mouse or by using the **Format** command on the toolbar.

To resize a column:

1. Select any cell in the column.
2. Click on the right edge of the column header and drag it to the right to widen the column.

To resize a row:

1. Click on any cell in the row.
2. Click on the bottom edge of the row header and drag it down to increase the height of the row.

Resizing Cells With The Format Command

You can also increase column width and row height of a range of cells at once by using the **Format** command button on the **Home** tab of the ribbon.

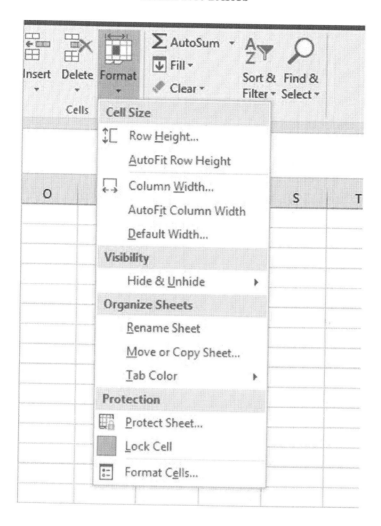

To increase the widths of columns A to E, for example:

1. Move your mouse pointer over the letter A until you see a downward pointing arrow.
2. Click on A to select the column and drag to column E to select columns A to E.

   Note: Another way to select a range of columns is to select the first column, hold down the SHIFT key, and select the last column.

3. Click on **Home > Format > Column Width**.

4. Enter the **Column width** in the box.
5. Click **OK**.

To increase the height of rows 1 to 14, for example:

1. Move your mouse pointer over the header of row 1 until you get an arrow pointing right.
2. Click to select the whole row.
3. Hold down the SHIFT key and click on the header of row 14.
4. Click on **Home** > **Format** > **Row Height...**
5. The default row height is 15. So, you can enter any number higher than 15 to increase the height of the selected rows.
6. Click **OK**.

Automatically adjust columns to fit your data using AutoFit

Select the columns you want to apply AutoFit to. Click on **Format** > **AutoFit Column Width**. This will adjust each column to fit the length of all entries.

Automatically adjust row heights to fit your data using AutoFit

Select the rows you want to apply AutoFit to. Select **Format** > **AutoFit Row Height.** This will adjust each column to fit the height of all entries. This is useful if you have **Wrap text** enabled and some cells have more than one line of text.

Set the default column width for the whole workbook

Select **Format** > **Default Width** and then enter the figure in the **Standard column width** box.

Hide Rows And Columns

On some occasions, you may want to hide some rows or columns to make your worksheet easier to read.

To hide **rows,** select the rows and then click on **Format**. On the pop-up menu, under **Visibility**, select **Hide & Unhide** and then select **Hide Rows**.

To hide **columns**, select the columns and then click on **Format**. On the pop-up menu, under **Visibility**, select **Hide & Unhide** and then select **Hide Columns**.

Unhide rows and columns

Navigate to **Home** > **Format** > **Hide & Unhide** and then select **Unhide Columns** to display hidden columns (or **Unhide Rows** to display hidden rows).

Hide And Unhide A Worksheet

You can use two methods to Hide a worksheet:

Method 1: Right-click on the worksheet's name tab and select **Hide** from the pop-up menu.

Method 2: Ensure the worksheet you want to hide is the active one, then select **Home** > **Format** > **Hide & Unhide** > **Hide Sheet**.

To Unhide a worksheet:

Method 1: Right-click on any of the tabs at the bottom of the workbook and select **Unhide** from the pop-up menu. Select the worksheet name in the **Unhide** window and click **OK**.

Method 2: Navigate to **Home** > **Format** > **Hide & Unhide** > **Unhide Sheet**. Select the sheet name from the list box and click **OK**.

Cell Styles

You can select a predefined colour format for your cells from a wide selection of styles from the **Styles** group on the **Home** tab.

To format a cell or range with a different style:

1. Select the cell or range.
2. Select **Home** > **Cell Styles**.
3. You can move your mouse pointer over the different styles to get a preview on your worksheet before you select one.
4. Select a style from the pop-up menu.

Merging Cells And Aligning Data

To **merge** cells on your worksheet, select the cells you want to merge. On the **Home** tab, click **Merge & Center**. Alternatively, you can click on the drop-down button for Merge & Center and choose other merge options from the pop-up menu.

To **unmerge** cells, select the merged cells, then on the **Home** tab, click on the drop-down button for **Merge & Center**. Select **Unmerge Cells** from the pop-up menu.

Text Alignment And Wrapping

To align text in a cell, select the cell and click on one of the alignment options in the **Alignment** group on the **Home** tab. You can also wrap text and merge cells from the command options available.

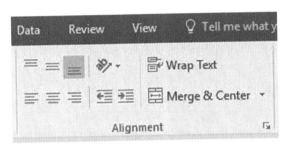

The **Format Cells** dialogue box provides additional formatting options like **Shrink to fit** and **Text direction**. To open the dialogue box, click on the dialogue box launcher on the bottom-right of the **Alignment** group.

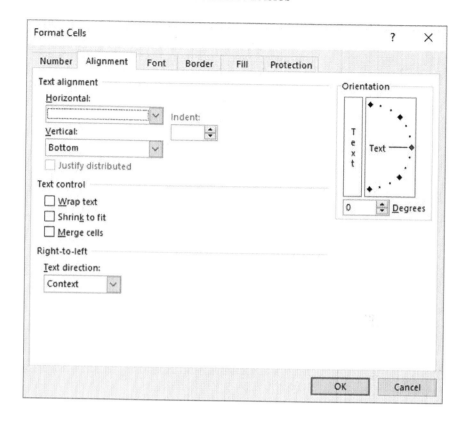

On the Alignment tab, you can:

1. Align text in your cells vertically and horizontally.
2. Wrap text so that it goes to a new line in a cell instead of continuing into other cells to the right.
3. Shrink text to fit one cell.
4. Merge cells.

Changing Number Formats

To set the number format for a range of cells:

1. Select the range of cells that you want to format.
2. On the **Home** tab, locate the **Number** group and click the drop-down list to display a pop-up menu with a list of formats.
3. Click on one of the formats. For example, *Currency* or *Short Date*.

Accessing More Number Formats

To choose a format that is not on the format drop-down list, for example, the currency of another country, click on the dialogue box launcher (the small diagonal arrow at the bottom-right of the **Number** group).

The **Format Cells** window will be displayed.

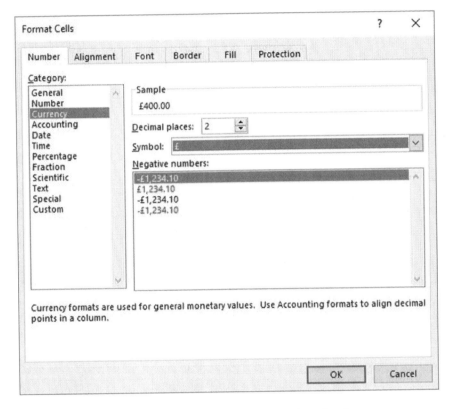

On the left side of the box under **Category**, select the format you want.

On the right side of the screen, you have several options that allow you to further configure your format. If you want to format your cells for a type of currency, select **Currency** from the list on the left and then from the **Symbol** drop-down list, select a currency sign. On this screen, you can also set the number of decimal places and the format you want for negative numbers.

The **Sample** field shows you how the chosen format will look on your worksheet.

Click **OK** to confirm your changes when done.

Creating Custom Numeric Formats

Excel has many built-in number formats you can use to create your own custom format if you can't find a predefined one for your needs.

Let's say you have a column in your worksheet that you use to record a set of numbers. It could be product serial numbers, unique product IDs, or even telephone numbers. You may want the numbers to appear in a certain format regardless of how they've been entered. In some applications like Microsoft Access, this would be called a *format mask*. In Excel, you can create your own format for a range so every entry is automatically formatted with your default format.

To create your own format:

1. Select the range of cells to be formatted.
2. Right-click any area in your selection and choose **Format Cells** from the pop-up menu. Alternatively, launch the **Format Cells** window by clicking the dialogue box launcher in the **Number** group on the **Home** tab.
3. Under **Category,** select **Custom.**

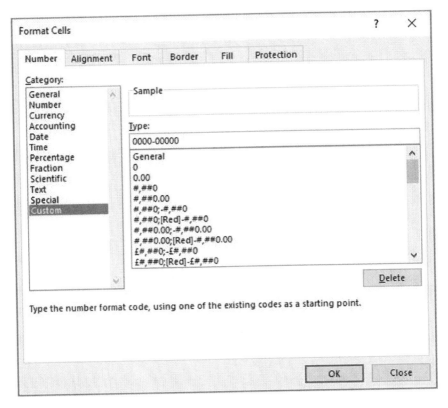

4. In the **Type** box, select an existing format close to the one you would like to create. **Note**: If you find a format on the list that meets your needs then you can just select that one and click OK.

5. In the Type box, type in the format you want to create. For example, *0000-00000*.

6. Click **OK**.

In the image below, column A has a set of numbers. Column B shows the same numbers with a custom format, *0000-00000*, now applied to them.

▲	A	B	C
1	**Serial Number**		
2	234401107	2344-01107	
3	234434589	2344-34589	
4	234466123	2344-66123	
5	234455692	2344-55692	
6	234234500	2342-34500	
7	234410976	2344-10976	
8	232310978	2323-10978	
9	234093419	2340-93419	
10	230923100	2309-23100	
11	234109035	2341-09035	
12	234102345	2341-02345	
13	234109093	2341-09093	
14			

The Format Painter

A quick way to format a cell or group of cells based on another cell is to use the **Format Painter**. This can be found in the **Clipboard** group on the **Home** tab.

To copy cell formatting with the Format Painter:
1. Click on the source cell, that is the cell you want to copy the format from.
2. Select **Home > Format Painter**. The mouse pointer will turn into a plus sign (+) and a brush icon.
3. Click and drag over the destination cells i.e. the cells you want to copy the format to. The destination cells will now have the same format as the source cell.

An Example:

If cell A2 is formatted as **Currency** and you want to format A3 to A14 as currency with the **Format Painter**, you would carry out the following steps:

1. Click on cell *A2* to select it.
2. Click on **Format Painter**.
3. Select *A3* to *A14*. Click *A3* and drag to *A14*. The currency format from *A2* will now be applied to *A3* - *A14*.

Clearing The Cell Format

To remove formatting from a cell or range, do the following:

1. Select the cells you want to clear.
2. Select **Home** > **Clear** (from the **Editing** group).
3. A pop-up menu with several options will be displayed - **Clear All, Clear Formats, Clear Contents, Clear Comments, and Clear Hyperlinks**.
4. To clear just the format and not the values, click on **Clear Formats**.

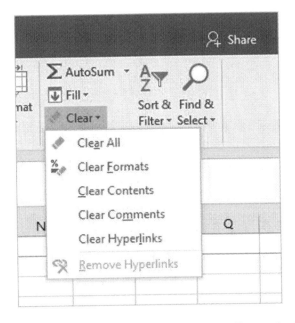

This will return the format of the selected cells to **General** which is the Excel default.

Add Data Validation To Cells

You can insert validation rules in cells to ensure that the data that is entered meets a certain criterion.

For example, let's say we want to create a list that will be used by many people. The list has the following columns: *Product Code*, *Product Name*, and *Price*. We want to insert a validation rule to ensure the *Product Code* is between 5 and 10 characters only. We could also specify whether we want numbers only, letters only, or a combination of both. For this example, we will make it a combination of letters and numbers.

Below is an example of how the list would look.

	A	B	C
1	Product Code	Product Name	Price
2	NWTB-1	Chai	$18.00
3	NWTCO-3	Syrup	$10.00
4	NWTCO-4	Cajun Seasoning	$22.00
5	NWTO-5	Olive Oil	$21.35
6	NWTJP-6	Boysenberry Spread	$25.00
7	NWTDFN-7	Dried Pears	$30.00
8	NWTS-8	Curry Sauce	$40.00
9	NWTDFN-14	Walnuts	$23.25
10	NWTCFV-17	Fruit Cocktail	$39.00
11	NWTBGM-19	Chocolate Biscuits Mix	$9.20
12	NWTJP-6	Marmalade	$81.00

How To Apply Validation Rules

Select the cells where you want to apply the rules.

Click on the **Data** tab in the ribbon, and under **Data Tools** you will find the **Data Validation** command.

Click on **Data Validation** to launch the Data Validation dialogue box. The box has three tabs, **Settings**, **Input Message**, and **Error Alert**.

On the **Settings** screen, the **Allow** box gives us several options including, **Text length**, **Whole number**, and **Decimal**.

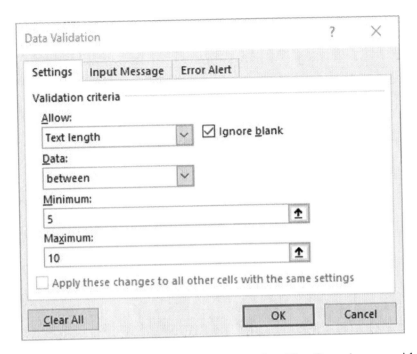

In the **Allow** box we choose **Text length**. The **Data** box provides several comparison operators we can use in our validation criteria. For this example, we want the *Product Code* to be no less than 5 characters and no more than 10 characters.

So, for our validation criteria we'll enter these entries:
- **Allow:** Text length
- **Data:** between
- **Minimum:** 5
- **Maximum:** 10

On the **Input Message** tab, we add a **Title** and the **Input message**. This help message will be displayed as a small pop-up when the user clicks on a cell with the validation rule.

For this example, we can add a message like:

"The Product Code can be alphanumeric and it should be between 5 and 10 characters."

In the **Error Alert** tab, we need to enter the message that is displayed when an entry fails the validation rule.

For the **Style,** we have 3 options. **Stop, Warning** and **Information.** We will choose the **Stop** icon for this example as a *Product Code* that does not meet the validation rule cannot be entered.

We can complete the **Title** and **Error Message** with the following:

Title: *"Invalid Entry!"*

Error Message: *"Invalid entry. Please enter a value between 5 and 10 characters in length."*

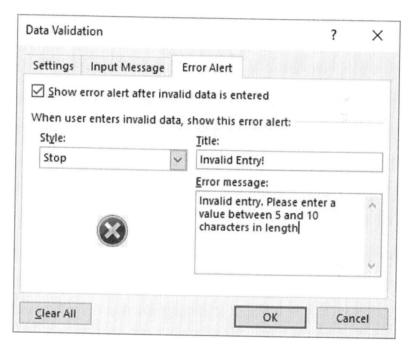

Once you have completed all the tabs click **OK.**

Data validation will now be applied to the selected cells.

How To Remove Data Validation From Cells

Occasionally you may want to change or remove data validation.
1. Select the cells where data validation has been applied.

2. On the **Data** tab, click on the **Data Validation** command to launch the Data Validation dialogue box.
3. To change the validation rule simply edit the various entries.
4. To remove the validation, click **Clear All**.

Click **OK**.

6 CARRYING OUT BASIC CALCULATIONS

Excel provides tools and features that enable you to carry out calculations of all kinds, from basic arithmetic to complex calculations using functions. In this chapter, we'll cover some of the most commonly used functions.

Arithmetic Operators

The following arithmetic operators are used to perform basic mathematical operations such as addition, subtraction, multiplication, or division.

Arithmetic operator	Meaning	Example
+ (plus sign)	Addition	=4+4
– (minus sign)	Subtraction	=4–4
	Negation	=-4
* (asterisk)	Multiplication	=4*4
/ (forward slash)	Division	=4/4
% (percent sign)	Percent	40 %
^ (caret)	Exponentiation	=4^4

Comparison Operators

Comparison operators allow you to compare two values and produce a logical result i.e. TRUE or FALSE.

Comparison operator	Meaning	Example
= (equal sign)	Equal to	=A1=B1
> (greater than sign)	Greater than	=A1>B1
< (less than sign)	Less than	=A1<B1
>= (greater than or equal to sign)	Greater than or equal to	=A1>=B1
<= (less than or equal to sign)	Less than or equal to	=A1<=B1
<> (not equal to sign)	Not equal to	=A1<>B1

Entering A Formula

To enter a formula in a cell, always start your entry with an equal sign (=) in the formula bar. This tells excel that your entry is a formula and not a static value.

Next to the formula bar, you have the **Enter** command (check mark) that you used to confirm your formula. So, you enter your formula in the formula bar and then click on **Enter** to confirm the entry. If you wish to **Cancel** the entry, then click on cancel to discard it.

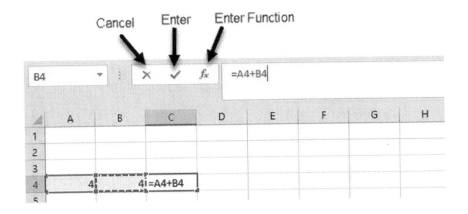

Let's say we want to add 2 figures 300 + 400.

1. Enter "300" in cell **A4**.
2. Enter "400" in cell **B4**.
3. In cell C4, enter "= A4 + B4".
4. Click on **Enter.**
5. C4 will now have the sum of the two figures which is 700.

To minimise errors, as much as possible avoid typing cell references directly in the formula bar. After you type in the equal sign (=) in the formula bar you can add cell references to your formula by selecting them from the worksheet with your mouse. Whenever you want to reference a cell, select the cell on the worksheet with your mouse to automatically enter its reference in the formula bar.

So, for the basic calculation we carried out above, the way you would enter it in the formula bar is as follows:

1. Select *C4*
2. Type "=" in the formula bar
3. Select on *A4*
4. Type "+"
5. Select *B4*
6. Click **Enter**

The sum of the 2 cells, "700", will now be displayed in cell C4.

Use Data From Other Worksheets In Formulas

On some occasions, you may be working on one worksheet and you want to access data on another worksheet in your formula. For example, your formula cell may be on Sheet1 and you want to reference a cell or range on **Sheet2** as part of the formula.

Let's say we want to create a formula in cell **A6 on Sheet1** and we want to grab a value from cell **A1 on Sheet2**:

1. Select A6 on Sheet1.
2. Type "= Sheet2!A1" in the formula bar.
3. Click **Enter.**

This will now include the cell from Sheet2 as part of your formula in A6 on Sheet1.

Another way to grab the cell reference is to simply select it with your mouse:

1. Select A6 on **Sheet1**.
2. Type "=" in the formula bar.
3. Click on the **Sheet2** tab (at the bottom of the screen).
4. Select cell A1 on Sheet2.
5. Click **Enter**.

The cell reference "Sheet2!A1" will automatically be entered in A6 on Sheet1.

The same method applies for a range. If you want to reference more than one cell i.e. a range, click on Sheet2 and select the range of cells, for example, A1:A10. The reference "Sheet2!A1:A10" will now be added to the formula bar in Sheet1.

7 THE AUTOSUM TOOL

The AutoSum tool can be found on the **Home** tab of the ribbon. It is the Greek Sigma symbol in the **Editing** group. AutoSum allows you to insert functions in your worksheet. The tool automatically selects the range to be used as the argument for you. You can calculate the SUM, AVERAGE, COUNT, MAX, and MIN functions.

A *range* in Excel is a collection of two or more cells that contain the data you're working with.

A function *argument* is simply a piece of data that a function needs to run. The SUM function, for example, can have one or more arguments for the input ranges to be summed.

=SUM(A2:A10)

=SUM(A2:A10, C2:C10)

The great thing about AutoSum is that it selects the most likely range of cells in the current column or row that you want to use. It then automatically enters them in the function's argument.

For the most part, it selects the correct range of cells and marks the selection with a moving dotted line called the *marquee*. On occasions where there are blank rows or columns in your data, i.e. the data is not continuous, AutoSum may not automatically select everything. In those cases, you can manually correct the range by dragging the cell pointer over the block of cells you want to calculate.

AutoSum will default to the SUM function when clicked. However, you can use a different function with AutoSum by clicking the drop-down button next to the AutoSum sign to display a pop-up menu of the other functions you can use. Click on one of them, for example, **Average**, to insert that as the function to be used with AutoSum.

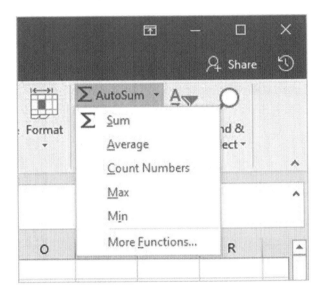

Let's say we have figures in B2 to B14 that we want to sum up. We can do so quickly using the AutoSum command.

| SUM | ▼ | ⋮ | × | ✓ | *fx* | =SUM(B2:B13) |

◢	A	B	C	D	E
1	**Month**	**Expenses**			
2	Jan	$400.00			
3	Feb	$500.00			
4	Mar	$300.00			
5	Apr	$700.00			
6	May	$800.00			
7	Jun	$750.00			
8	Jul	$800.00			
9	Aug	$600.00			
10	Sep	$550.00			
11	Oct	$420.00			
12	Nov	$350.00			
13	Dec	$800.00			
14	**Sum**	=SUM(B2:B13)			
15		SUM(**number1**, [number2], ...)			
16					

1. Click on the cell where you want the total displayed. For this example, this would be **B14**.
2. Click the **AutoSum** command button (**Home** > **Editing** group > **AutoSum**).
3. AutoSum will automatically select the range of cells with continuous data (above or to the side of the cell with the formula). In this case, it selects B2 to B13.
4. Click **Enter** (the check mark next to the formula bar).

Cell B14 will now show the sum of the numbers.

Using AutoSum With A Non-Contiguous Range

A non-contiguous range has blank rows or columns in the data. AutoSum will only select the contiguous range next to the cell with the formula so you must manually drag the selection over the rest of the data.

1. Click on the cell where you want the total to be displayed.
2. Click the **AutoSum** command button.
3. AutoSum will automatically select the range of cells next to the cell with the formula.
4. Place your mouse pointer at the edge of the selection (over the cell pointer) until it turns into a double-headed arrow. Drag it over the rest of the cells in your range.
5. Click **Enter**.

The formula cell will now show the sum of the numbers.

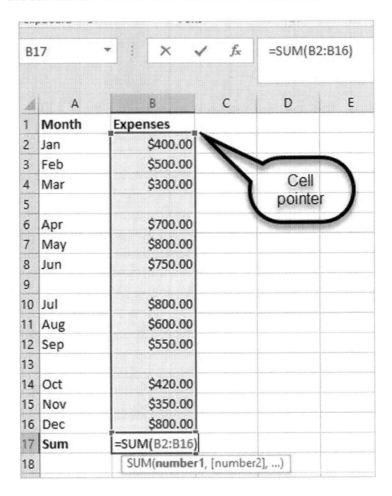

Using AutoSum With Different Ranges

Sometimes the data you want to calculate may be in different parts of the worksheet or even on different worksheets. With AutoSum, you can calculate individual values, cell references, ranges, or a mix of all three.

Summing up values in different ranges:

1. Click on the cell where you want the formula and then click on **AutoSum**.
2. If AutoSum does not select the first range for you then select it by clicking on the first cell and dragging to the last cell of the range.
3. Hold down the **CTRL** key and select any additional ranges you want to add to the calculation.
4. Click **Enter**.

D3		✕ ✓ f_x	=SUM(B3:B8,D3:D8)				
	A	B	C	D	E	F	G
1							
2		Month 1		Month 2			
3	Jane	$1,000.00		$1,100.00			
4	Peter	$2,000.00		$1,500.00			
5	Derek	$1,000.00		$1,200.00			
6	Jason	$1,100.00		$1,300.00			
7	Mark	$1,500.00		$1,600.00			
8	Julie	$1,200.00		$1,300.00			
9							
10							
11	Total		=SUM(B3:B8,D3:D8)				
12			SUM(number1, [number2], [number3], ...)				
13							

The sum of both ranges will now be entered. You can include up to 255 ranges as arguments in your SUM function.

Using AutoSum For Other Functions

As mentioned previously, you can use AutoSum to calculate the Average, Count, Max, and Min. To select these other functions, click on the drop-down arrow on the AutoSum command and select one of them.

For example, to calculate the average of a row of numbers in cells B4 to I4, you would do the following:

1. Select the cell where you want to display the average. This will be J4 for this example.
2. Select **AutoSum** > **Average**.
3. AutoSum will automatically select all the contiguous cells next to the formula cell. For this example, it will be B4 to I4.
4. Click on **Enter**

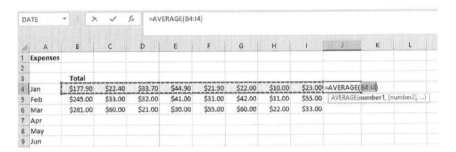

The average for B4:I4 will now be calculated and displayed in J4.

Quick Sum With The Status Bar

If you want to quickly see the sum of the range of cells select the range and view the information on the Status Bar. To select a range of cells, click on the first cell, and hold down the SHIFT key, then click on the last cell in the range.

Once you have selected the range, look at the lower right-hand side of the Excel **Status Bar**. You will see displayed, the **Average**, **Count**, and **Sum** for the cells you have selected.

	Month 1
Jane	$1,000.00
Peter	$2,000.00
Derek	$1,000.00
Jason	$1,100.00
Mark	$1,500.00
Julie	$1,200.00

Average: $1,300.00   Count: 6   Sum: $7,800.00

8 WORKING WITH FUNCTIONS

In the examples above we've seen how we can apply SUM and some other functions with the AutoSum tool. You can also enter the functions without using AutoSum, especially if your calculation is more complex, involving data from many parts of the worksheet or even across multiple worksheets. You can use functions to calculate raw values, cell references, ranges, or a mix of all three.

The SUM Function

Let's say you have values in cells B2 to B13 that you want to sum up.

| SUM | ▼ | ⋮ | ✕ | ✓ | *fx* | =SUM(B2:B13) |

◢	A	B	C	D	E
1	**Month**	**Expenses**			
2	Jan	$400.00			
3	Feb	$640.00			
4	Mar	$550.00			
5	Apr	$420.00			
6	May	$310.50			
7	Jun	$566.30			
8	Jul	$607.90			
9	Aug	$300.80			
10	Sep	$500.50			
11	Oct	$700.00			
12	Nov	$840.00			
13	Dec	$900.00			
14	**Sum**	=SUM(B2:B13)			
15		SUM(**number1**, [number2], ...)			
16					

Summing contiguous data:
1. Select the cell you want to use for the sum. In this case it is B14.
2. Click in the formula bar and enter "=SUM(".
3. Select B2 and drag down to B13.
4. Type ")" in the formula bar to close the bracket.
5. Click **Enter**.

Summing non-contiguous data:
1. Select the cell where you want to place the formula.
2. Click in the formula bar and type in the function name with the opening bracket. For example "=SUM(".
3. Select the first range.
4. Type in a comma i.e. "=SUM(B2:B13,".
5. Select the next range and type in a comma.
6. Select any additional ranges, making sure you type a comma after each range.

7. Type in the closing bracket. You should now have something like this: "*=SUM(B2:B13,D2:D13,F2:F13,H2:H13)*".
8. Click **Enter** (check mark).

The IF Function

The IF function is one of the most popular functions in Excel. It allows you to use comparison operators to evaluate values and return different results based on the result of the evaluation.

In its simplest form this is what the function says:
If (something is TRUE, then do A, otherwise do B)

So, the IF statement will return a different result for TRUE and FALSE.
A simple way it is commonly used is to determine if a calculated cell has any value or not. If the result is 0 then it returns a blank cell.

In the example below, the formula for the total for **Jan** was entered in cell **B4** and dragged down to populate the totals for **Feb** to **Dec.** This ensures those months are automatically calculated in the future, when their figures are entered.

Thus, the formula for **Apr** in cell B7 is:

=IF(SUM(C7:I7) > 0,SUM(C7:I7),"")

Without the IF function, it would display $0 for the unpopulated months, however, we want the totals for the unpopulated months to be blank instead of $0.

| B7 | | ▾ | : | × | ✓ | *fx* | =IF(SUM(C7:I7) > 0,SUM(C7:I7),"") | | |

▲	A	B	C	D	E	F	G	H	I
1	Expenses								
2									
3		**Total**							
4	Jan	$177.90	$22.40	$33.70	$44.90	$21.90	$22.00	$10.00	$23.00
5	Feb	$245.00	$33.00	$32.00	$41.00	$31.00	$42.00	$11.00	$55.00
6	Mar	$281.00	$60.00	$21.00	$30.00	$55.00	$60.00	$22.00	$33.00
7	Apr								
8	May								
9	Jun								
10	Jul								
11	Aug								
12	Sep								
13	Oct								
14	Nov								
15	Dec								

The IF function in this example checks to see if the sum in *column B* is greater than zero. If true it returns the sum. If it is false then it returns a blank string.

In another example, we could use the results of an evaluation to return different values in our worksheet.

Let's say we have a budgeting sheet and want to use a "Status" column to report on how the **Actual** figure compares to the **Budgeted** figure. In this case, we can use the IF statement to test whether the actual figure is greater than the budgeted figure. If **Actual** is greater than **Budgeted**, the formula would enter "Over Budget", otherwise it would enter "Within Budget".

| C2 | ▼ | : | × | ✓ | *fₓ* | =IF(B2 > A2,"Over Budget", "Within Budget") |

◢	A	B	C	D	E	F	G
1	**Budgeted**	**Actual**	**Status**				
2	$1,000.00	$900.00	Within Budget				
3	$2,000.00	$1,100.00	Within Budget				
4	$2,500.00	$1,500.00	Within Budget				
5	$2,300.00	$2,100.00	Within Budget				
6	$1,500.00	$2,300.00	Over Budget				
7	$1,200.00	$2,100.00	Over Budget				
8	$2,050.00	$2,030.00	Within Budget				
9	$5,000.00	$4,100.00	Within Budget				
10	$3,000.00	$2,100.00	Within Budget				
11							

=IF(B2 > A2,"Over Budget", "Within Budget")

The IF function checks to see if the value in B2 is greater than the value in A2. If it is, it returns "Over Budget" otherwise it returns "Within Budget".

The DATE Function

The date function in Excel is a popular function used to calculate and manipulate dates.

The syntax for the Date function is:

DATE (year, month, day)

For example, the DATE function will return *11/4/2017* when given the following argument DATE (2017, 11, 04).

D2	▼	⋮	✕	✓	*fx*	=DATE(C2,A2,B2)

◢	A	B	C	D	E
1	Day	Month	Year	Combined Date	
2	4	11	2017	4/11/2017	
3					
4					

Note: This date is in the format: *Day/Month/Year.*

You can use the DATE function to calculate a date based on another date.

For example, you can combine the YEAR, MONTH, and DAY functions within the DATE function to calculate a new date based on another date.

Let's say you want to maintain a spreadsheet that keeps track of the end dates of many 5-year contracts. The *start dates* are in column A and the *end dates* in column B.

The DATE function can be used to automatically establish the *end date* as soon as a *start date* is entered:

B3	▼	⋮	✕	✓	*fx*	=DATE(YEAR(A3)+5,MONTH(A3),DAY(A3))

◢	A	B	C	D	E	F	G
1	Contracts						
2	Start Date	End Date					
3	25/01/2015	25/01/2020					
4	01/04/2016	01/04/2021					
5	01/02/2017	01/02/2022					
6							

Calculate a date based on another date:

The DATE function creates a date from the formula:

=DATE(YEAR(A3)+5,MONTH(A3),DAY(A3))

- The **YEAR** function looks at cell A3 and extracts "2015". It then, adds 5 years and returns 2020 as the end year.
- The **MONTH** function extracts the "4" from A3 and returns "4" as the month in cell B3.
- The **DAY** function extracts 25 from A3 and returns 25 as the day in cell B3.

The DATEDIF Function

This function calculates the number of days, months, or years between two dates. It is one of the legacy functions in Excel but it still works and is a faster way for working out the difference between two dates.

Syntax:

DATEDIF (*start_date, end_date, unit*)

start_date: This argument represents the start date of the period.

end_date: This argument represents the end date of the period.

Unit: This can be Y, M, D, YM, or YD.

Unit	Returns
"Y"	Calculates the number of years in the period.
"M"	Calculates the number of months in the period.
"D"	Calculates the number of days in the period.
"YM"	Calculates the difference between the months in start_date and end_date. The days and years of the dates are ignored.
"YD"	Calculates the difference between the days of start_date and end_date. The years of the dates are ignored.

Note: There is also an "MD" argument that calculates the number of days while ignoring the month and years. I have not included it here as Microsoft no longer recommends the use of this argument due to known limitations. Under certain conditions it could return a negative number.

The DATEDIF function comes in handy when you need to calculate an age, for example.

In the example below, it was easy to calculate the age of someone born in 1980.

C1			×	✓	f_x	=DATEDIF(A1,B1,"Y")

	A	B	C	D	E
1	01/01/1980	11/04/2017	37		
2					
3					

The DAYS Function

The DAYS function calculates the number of days between two given dates.

Syntax:

DAYS (end_date, start_date)

The start_date and end_date are the two dates between which you want to calculate the number of days.

For example:

DAYS (01/01/2018, 01/01/2017) will return 365 days.

The VLOOKUP Function

The VLOOKUP function allows you to find one piece of information in a spreadsheet based on another piece of information.

VLOOKUP (lookup_value, table_array, col_index_num, [range_lookup])

Description of arguments:

- **Lookup_value:** What value are you searching for? This is the lookup value. Excel will look for a match to this value in the leftmost column of your chosen range.

- **Table_array:** What columns do you want to search? This is the lookup table containing all the columns you want to include in your search.
- **Col_index_num:** Which column contains the search result? Count from the first column to determine what this number should be, starting from 1.
- **Range_lookup:** If you want an exact match, enter FALSE or 0 here. Alternatively, if an approximate match is OK then enter TRUE or 1. For TRUE, you would need to sort the leftmost column in ascending order for correct results. This is an optional argument and if left out it will default to TRUE.

In the example below, we use VLOOPUP to find the *Price* of a product by giving it the *Product Name* in cell G2. The formula is in cell G3 and as you can see from the image below, it searches the tables for *Dried Pears* and returns the price from the next column.

=VLOOKUP(G2, B2:D46, 2, FALSE)

The function uses a **lookup_value** from cell "G2" to search a **table_array** which is "B2:D46".

The **col_index_num** is "2" so it returns a value from the second column in the table array, which is the *Price* column.

The **range_lookup** is "FALSE" meaning we want an exact match

Accessing More Functions From The Formulas Tab
To access more functions in Excel, click on the **Formulas** tab on the ribbon. You will see a list of command buttons for several categories of functions.

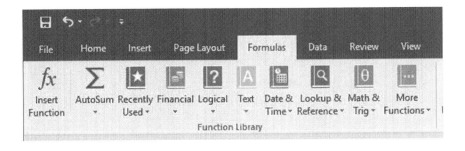

These are grouped under:

1. Recently Used
2. Financial
3. Logical
4. Text
5. Date and Time.
6. Lookup & Reference.
7. Math & Trig
8. More Functions

You can explore the various functions by clicking on the drop-down button for each one of the command buttons and you'll get a pop-up list of the functions related to each button.

Most people will never get to use most of these functions as many of them are for specialised tasks and professions, so don't let them overwhelm you. For example, the **Financial** functions are mostly going to be used by accountants. The **Math & Trig** functions are mostly going to be used by scientists and mathematicians.

The ones you use the most will be listed under the **Recently Used** list for easy access.

To get more details about each function, simply move your mouse pointer over a function name on the list and a small pop-up box will appear to give you more details of the function and what arguments it takes. For example, if you move your mouse pointer over the **IF** function, you will see the function description and the arguments it takes.

Another way to use functions is to click on the **Insert Function** command button, which is the first command button on the **Formulas** tab.

When you click on this button, you will get the **Insert Function** window that allows you to select the category of function you want. A list of the functions within that category will be displayed in the list box below.

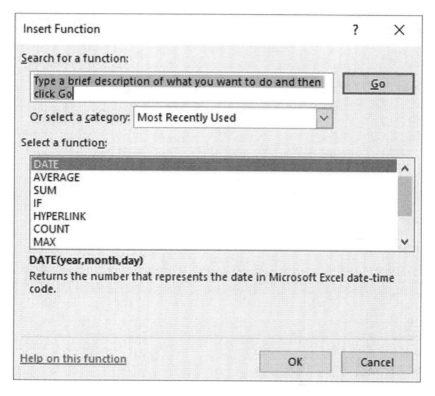

When you select a function from the list and click **OK** it displays a **Function Arguments** dialogue box which gives you several boxes to enable you to build your formula.

Getting More Help With Functions

To get more information on the use of any function in Excel, press **F1** to display the Help panel. Then type "Excel functions" in the search bar. This will give you a list of all the functions in Excel by category. You can locate the one you want and click on it to see more details on how it is used.

9 WORKING WITH TABLES

You can turn your Excel data into a table. When you create a table in Excel it is easier for you to manage and analyse your data. You also get built-in sorting, filtering, Banded Rows, and the ability to add a Total Row.

Before you create a table ensure there are no empty columns or rows in the data.

In the next example, we will convert the following range of data into a table.

	A	B	C	D	E
1	Last Name	First Name	Company	Job Title	Address
2	Bedecs	Anna	Company A	Owner	123 1st Street
3	Gratacos Solsona	Antonio	Company B	Owner	123 2nd Stree
4	Axen	Thomas	Company C	Purchasing Represen	123 3rd Street
5	Lee	Christina	Company D	Purchasing Manager	123 4th Street
6	O'Donnell	Martin	Company E	Owner	123 5th Street
7	Pérez-Olaeta	Francisco	Company F	Purchasing Manager	123 6th Street
8	Xie	Ming-Yang	Company G	Owner	123 7th Street
9	Andersen	Elizabeth	Company H	Purchasing Represen	123 8th Street
10	Mortensen	Sven	Company I	Purchasing Manager	123 9th Street
11	Wacker	Roland	Company J	Purchasing Manager	123 10th Street
12	Krschne	Peter	Company K	Purchasing Manager	123 11th Stree
13	Edwards	John	Company L	Purchasing Manager	123 12th Stree
14	Ludick	Andre	Company M	Purchasing Represen	456 13th Stree
15	Grilo	Carlos	Company N	Purchasing Represen	456 14th Street
16	Kupkova	Helena	Company O	Purchasing Manager	456 15th Stree

First, check that there are no empty columns and rows in your data:

1. Select a cell within the data and press "CTRL" + "A".
2. Then press "CTRL" + "." a few times to move around the data.

Note: "CTRL" + "A" selects the data range in question. "CTRL" + "." moves around the four edges of the data so you can see where the data starts and ends.

To create a table from your data:

1. Click on any cell within the data.
2. Click on the **Insert** tab and click on **Table** (in the **Tables** group).
3. A dialogue box will be displayed showing you the range to be used for the table. You can adjust the range here if necessary.
4. Click on the **My table has headers** check box to ensure that the first row of your table is used as the header.

Note: if your table has no headers. It is best to add a row with headers as this makes it easier to work with tables in Excel.

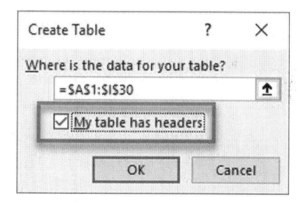

5. Click OK.

The table will be created with your first row used as column headers.

	A	B	C	D	E
1	Last Name	First Name	Company	Job Title	Address
2	Bedecs	Anna	Company A	Owner	123 1st Street
3	Gratacos Solsona	Antonio	Company B	Owner	123 2nd Street
4	Axen	Thomas	Company C	Purchasing Represen	123 3rd Street
5	Lee	Christina	Company D	Purchasing Manager	123 4th Street
6	O'Donnell	Martin	Company E	Owner	123 5th Street
7	Pérez-Olaeta	Francisco	Company F	Purchasing Manager	123 6th Street
8	Xie	Ming-Yang	Company G	Owner	123 7th Street
9	Andersen	Elizabeth	Company H	Purchasing Represen	123 8th Street
10	Mortensen	Sven	Company I	Purchasing Manager	123 9th Street
11	Wacker	Roland	Company J	Purchasing Manager	123 10th Street
12	Krschne	Peter	Company K	Purchasing Manager	123 11th Street
13	Edwards	John	Company L	Purchasing Manager	123 12th Street
14	Ludick	Andre	Company M	Purchasing Represen	456 13th Street
15	Grilo	Carlos	Company N	Purchasing Represen	456 14th Street
16	Kupkova	Helena	Company O	Purchasing Manager	456 15th Street

Another way to format a range as a table is to select the cells in the range and on the ribbon, select **Home > Format as Table.**

Choosing A Style For Your Table

When you convert a range to a table, you will notice that a style with alternating row colours has been applied to the table. You can change this style if you want by selecting a new style from many options provided by Excel.

To format your table with a Style:

1. Select a cell within the table.
2. On the **Design** tab, locate the **Table Styles** group and click on the drop-down button for the styles. A drop-down menu will show you more styles.
3. Move your mouse pointer over each style to see a preview of how it would look on your worksheet.
4. When you find a style, click on it to apply it to your table.

Table Style Options

On the **Design** tab, you'll find a group, **Table style options**, that provides several options for configuring the style of your table.

For example, you can change your table from Banded Row to Banded Columns. Banded rows are the alternating colours applied to your table rows. Banded Rows is the default but if you want banded columns instead, uncheck **Banded Rows** and check **Banded Columns** to have your columns alternate in colour instead of your row.

Note that if a new column or row is added to the table, it will automatically inherit the current table style. When you add a new row, any formulas applied to your table will also be copied to the new row.

Sorting Data In A Table

Before you begin sorting data, ensure there are no blank rows and blank columns.

To check this, select a cell within the data and press "CTRL" + "A". Then press "CTRL" + "." a few times. It moves the cursor around the four corners of the range so you can see the whole area.

Before you start sorting, also make sure your table header is a single row. If it is made up of more than one row then change it to a single row because it will make things a lot easier.

Sort Data Using One Column

To quickly sort using one column in your table, select a cell in the column you want to use for the sorting, for example, *Last Name*. Click on the **Data** tab on the ribbon. Click **AZ** (for ascending order) or **ZA** (for descending order) in the **Sort & Filter** group.

Sort Data Using Multiple Columns

1. Select a cell within the data. Click on **Home > Sort & Filter,** or click on **Data > Sort**.

You'll get a pop-up menu with three sort options:

- **Sort A to Z** – this option sorts the selected column in an ascending order.

- **Sort Z to A** – this option sorts the selected column in a descending order.

- **Custom Sort** – allows you to sort data in multiple columns using different sort criteria.

2. **Custom Sort** is required for multiple columns so click on **Custom Sort** on the menu. The sort dialogue box will be displayed.

3. Click on **Add Level**.

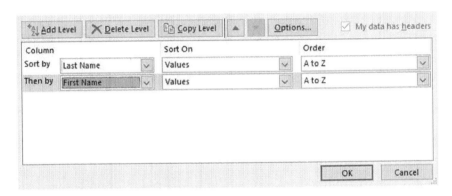

4. Under **Column**, select the column you want to **Sort by** from the drop-down list.

5. Select the second column you want to include in the sort in the **Then by** field. For example, Sort by Last Name and First Name.

6. Under **Sort On**, select **Values**. Under **Order**, select the order you want to sort on i.e. **A to Z** for ascending order, and **Z to A** for descending order.

7. Click **OK** when done.

You can add additional columns to your sort. Starting with Excel 2016 you can have up to 64 sort levels.

For each additional column that you want to sort by, repeat steps 4-7 above.

Filtering Your Data

Excel 2016 provides an array of options to filter your data so that you can view data that meets a certain criterion. Filters provide a quick way to work with a subset of data in a table or range. When you apply the filter you temporarily hide some of the data so that you can focus on the data you need to view.

How to filter data:

1. Select a cell within the data that you want to filter.
2. Click on **Home** > **Sort & Filter** > **Filter** (or select **Data** > **Filter**).
3. You will get filter arrows at the top of each column.
4. Click the filter drop-down arrow of the column you want to filter. For example, Price.
5. Uncheck **Select All**, and check the values you want to use for the filter.
6. Click **OK**.

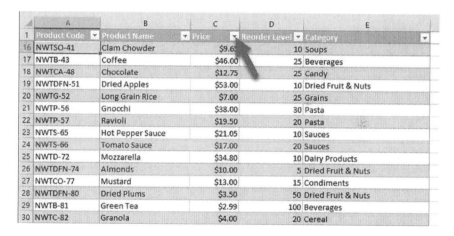

	A	B	C	D	E
1	Product Code	Product Name	Price	Reorder Level	Category
16	NWTSO-41	Clam Chowder	$9.65	10	Soups
17	NWTB-43	Coffee	$46.00	25	Beverages
18	NWTCA-48	Chocolate	$12.75	25	Candy
19	NWTDFN-51	Dried Apples	$53.00	10	Dried Fruit & Nuts
20	NWTG-52	Long Grain Rice	$7.00	25	Grains
21	NWTP-56	Gnocchi	$38.00	30	Pasta
22	NWTP-57	Ravioli	$19.50	20	Pasta
23	NWTS-65	Hot Pepper Sauce	$21.05	10	Sauces
24	NWTS-66	Tomato Sauce	$17.00	20	Sauces
25	NWTD-72	Mozzarella	$34.80	10	Dairy Products
26	NWTDFN-74	Almonds	$10.00	5	Dried Fruit & Nuts
27	NWTCO-77	Mustard	$13.00	15	Condiments
28	NWTDFN-80	Dried Plums	$3.50	50	Dried Fruit & Nuts
29	NWTB-81	Green Tea	$2.99	100	Beverages
30	NWTC-82	Granola	$4.00	20	Cereal

The filter drop-down arrow changes to a funnel icon to show that the column is filtered. If you look at the row heading numbers you'll see that they're now blue, indicating which rows are included in the filtered data.

To remove the filter, click on **Clear** in the **Sort & Filter** group. The filter will be removed and all data will be displayed.

Applying A Custom Filter

Select the filter drop-down arrow and then select one from the following:

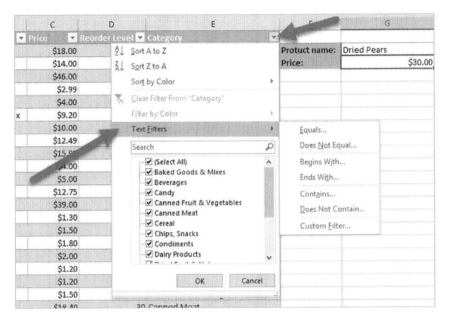

- **Text Filters** - this is available when the column has a text field or has a mixture of text and numbers: Equals, Does Not Equal, Begins With, Ends With, or Contains.
- **Number Filters** - this option is only available when the column contains only numbers: Equals, Does Not Equal, Greater Than, Less Than, or Between.
- **Date Filters** - this option is only available when the column contains only dates: Last Week, Next Month, This Month, and Last Month.
- **Clear Filter from 'Column name'** - this option is only available if a filter has already been applied to the column. Select this option to clear the filter.

When you select any of the first 3 options you will get a dialogue box – **Custom AutoFilter**.

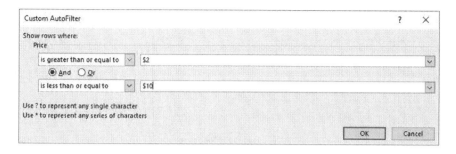

Select **And** if both conditions must be true. Alternatively, select **Or** if only one of the conditions needs to be true.

Enter the values you want to use for the filter.

For example, to view rows with a number that is within a certain range, select **Number Filters > Between** and then enter the values in the two boxes provided.

For the example in the image above, we're filtering the *Price* column so that only rows between $2 and $10 are shown.

To change the order of the filtered results, click the filter drop-down button, and then select either **Sort Largest to Smallest** or **Sort Smallest to Largest**.

For a text sort column, it would be **Sort A to Z** or **Sort Z to A**.

Adding A Totals Row To Your Table

You can add totals to a table by selecting the **Total Row** check box on the **Design** tab. Once added to your worksheet, the Total Row drop-down button allows you to add a function from a list of options.

To add totals to your table:

1. Select a cell in a table.
2. Select **Design > Total Row**. A new row is added to the bottom of the table. This is called the **Total Row**.
3. On the total row drop-down list, you have a choice of functions to select from, like Average, Count, Count Numbers, Max, Min, Sum, StdDev, Var, and more.

NWTS-65	Hot Pepper Sauce	$21.05		10	Sauces
NWTS-66	Tomato Sauce	$17.00		20	Sauces
NWTS-8	Curry Sauce	$40.00		10	Sauces
NWTSO-41	Clam Chowder	$9.65		10	Soups
NWTSO-98	Vegetable Soup	$1.89		100	Soups
NWTSO-99	Chicken Soup	$1.95		100	Soups
Total		$713.06 ▾			

None
Average
Count
Count Numbers
Max
Min
Sum
StdDev
Var
More Functions...

Note: If you need to add a new row of data to your table at some later point you need to uncheck **Total Row** on the **Design** tab, add the new row, and then recheck **Total Row**.

10 CREATING CHARTS WITH EXCEL

Excel charts provide a way to present your data visually. As the saying goes, *a picture is worth a thousand words*. Some of us don't absorb numbers as easily as others because we're more visual and this is where charts come in. A visual representation may sometimes create more of an impact with your audience.

To quickly create a chart from your data:

1. Select the range for your chart. Make sure you leave out any rows with totals from the selection.
2. Select **Insert > Recommended Charts**. This will open the **Insert Chart** dialogue box with 2 tabs - **Recommended Charts** and **All Charts**.
3. Select a chart on the Recommended Charts tab. For example, the second one, **Clustered Column**, which is one of the most common one used.
4. Click OK.

A floating chat will be created in the same worksheet as your data. You can click and drag this chart to another part of the screen if necessary.

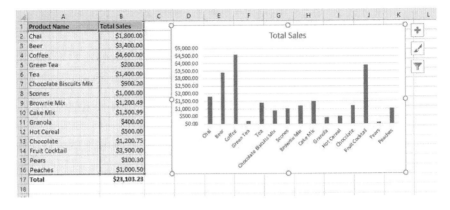

To delete a chart, simply select the chart and press delete.

Note that after creating the chart you'll get a new tab on the ribbon called **Design**. This tab provides many options to edit and style your chart.

Using The Quick Analysis Tool

The Quick Analysis tool offers a host of features for quickly adding conditional formatting, charts, totals, tables and sparklines to your worksheet tables.

In the following example, we'll use the Quick Analysis tool to add sparklines to our worksheet. Sparklines are mini-charts you can place in single cells to show the visual trend of your data. Excel 2016 allows you to quickly add Sparkline charts to your worksheet in a few steps.

Adding a Sparkline:

1. Select the data you want to create a Sparkline chart for. At the lower-right corner of the selection, you'll see the **Quick Analysis** tool.
2. Click on the Quick Analysis tool to open a pop-up menu of Quick Analysis options - **Formatting**, **Charts**, **Totals**, **Tables**, and **Sparklines**.
3. Click on SparkLines and then select one option from **Line**, **Column**, or **Win/Loss**.

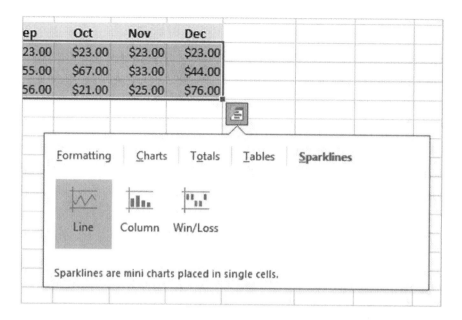

For this example, I have selected the **Line** option. The SparkLines will be created in the cells to the right of the selected values.

Formatting A Sparkline Chart

To format your Sparkline chart, click on it to select it.

1. Click on the **Design** tab on the ribbon, and in the **Style** group. You get various options to edit and style your Sparkline chart.

2. Use the following options to design your Sparkline:

- Click on **Line**, **Column**, or **Win/Loss** to change the chart type.

- You can check **Markers** to highlight specific values in the Sparkline chart.

- You can select a different **Style** for the Sparkline.

- You can change the **Sparkline Color** and the **Marker Color**.

- Click on **Sparkline Color** > **Weight** to change the width of the Sparkline.

- Click on **Marker Color** to change the colour of the markers.

- Click on **Axis** to show the axis, if the data has positive and negative values.

Customising Your Chart

To change the title, layout, chart style and theme colour of your chart, you can use Excel's formatting options.

Let's say we need to create a chart with four quarters of sales.

▲	A	B	C	D	E	
1	Sales by Quarter					
2	Product	QTR1	QTR2	QTR3	QTR4	
3	Chai	300	300	200	400	
4	Beer	300	200	400	300	
5	Coffee	350	400	500	500	
6	Green Tea	250	150	100	300	
7	Tea	100	400	100	500	
8	Chocolate Biscu	320	200	100	300	
9	Scones	250	500	200	100	
10	Brownie Mix	350	400	550	200	
11	Cake Mix	200	370	300	200	
12	Granola	250	100	200	400	
13	Hot Cereal	350	500	300	200	
14	Chocolate	350	200	500	500	
15	Fruit Cocktail	200	230	250	200	
16	Pears	100	200	300	450	
17	Peaches	200	300	200	600	
18						

To create the chart:

1. Select the range with the data, including the column headers and row headers.
2. Click on **Insert > Recommended Charts.** You're presented with the **Insert Chart** dialogue box with several chart recommendations for your data.
3. Select the **Clustered Column** option.
4. Click **OK.**

A chart will be created and added to your worksheet.

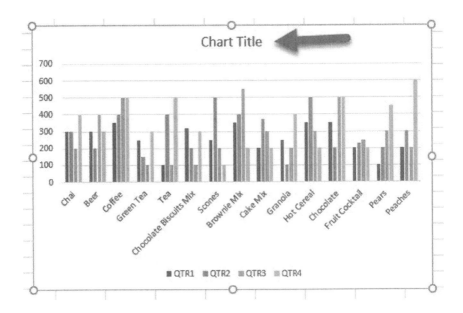

You can see from the chart that "Chart Title" is a placeholder that needs to be edited with the title of the chart. There are also no labels at the axis and we may want to add them to the chart.

To change the **Chart Title,** you can click on it and type in the title. Alternatively, you can select the name from a field on your worksheet. For example, if we wanted our chart title to be *Sales by quarter,* which is in cell **A1** of our worksheet, we would click on Chart Title and in the formula bar, enter "**=A1**".

Adding Axis Titles

We can also add titles down the left-hand side and at the bottom of the chart. These are called axis titles. The left side is the *y*-axis while the bottom is the *x*-axis.

To change the layout of your chart, click on **Design > Quick Layout**.

You'll get a pop-up with several chart layouts. You can move your mouse pointer over each layout to view more details about it. A few of the options provide axis titles as well as moving the legend to the right of the chart. If you want a layout with both axis titles then **Layout 9** would be a good pick.

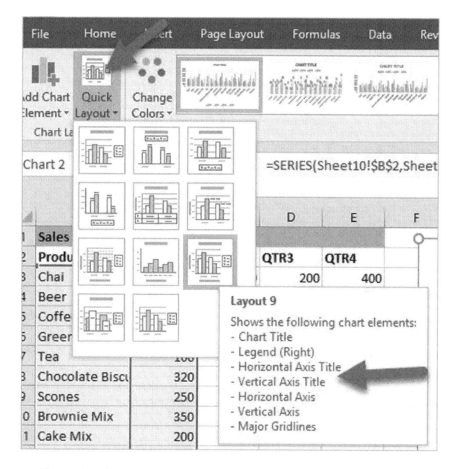

If we select **Layout 9** we get a chart with labels that we can edit to add titles to the x and y-axis.

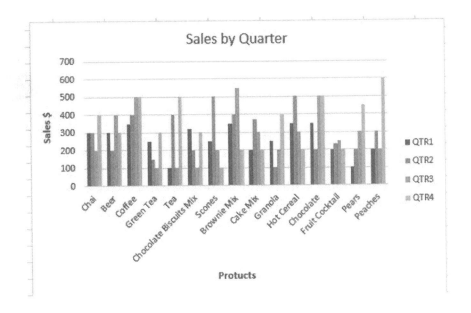

Chart Styles

When you click on the chart, the **Design** tab shows up on the ribbon. On this tab, you have an array of **Chart Styles** you can choose from to change the look and colour of your chart.

To change the colour of the plot area:

1. Click on the plot area to select it (this is the centre of the chart).
2. Click on the **Format** tab on the ribbon.
3. Click the drop-down button in the **Shape Styles** group.
4. You'll get a pop-up with many **Theme Styles** to choose from for the format of your plot area. You can move your mouse pointer over each one to see a preview of how your chart would look with it selected.
5. When you find the one you want, click on it to select it.

11 PRINTING YOUR WORKSHEET

The world is increasingly becoming paperless, however, on some occasions, you may need to print out a hardcopy of your worksheet. You may want to print it as part of a report or to share with others. Excel provides a rich array of features that allows you to print your data in many ways.

Set the Orientation to Landscape

The landscape orientation is best for printing worksheets unless you have specific reasons to use portrait.

On the **Page Layout** tab click on **Orientation** and select **Landscape**.

How To Set the Print Area

You need to set the **Print Area** so that blank pages are not included in the print.

1. Select the area in the worksheet that contains the data you want to print.
2. On the **Page Layout** tab, click on **Print Area.**
3. Select **Set Print Area**.

Note: To clear the print area click on **Print Area** and select **Clear Print Area**.

To Print Your Worksheet:

1. Click on **File** > **Print**.

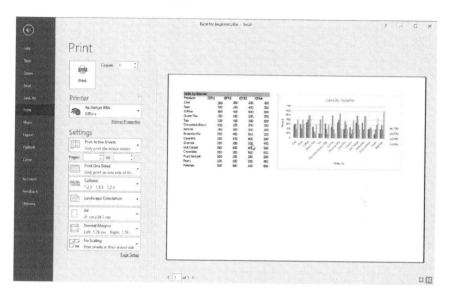

2. Print Active Sheet should be selected by default. Leave it like this if you want to print only the active worksheet. If your workbook has more than one worksheet and you want you print them all then click on the drop-down list and select **Print Entire Workbook** from the list.

3. If you haven't set the orientation to landscape yet, you can change it here.

4. Select the scaling option. There are several scaling options available:

   - **No Scaling** - the document will be printed as is, even if it carries on into other pages.
   - **Fit Sheet on One Page** – all columns and rows in the print area will be scaled into one page.
   - **Fit All Columns on One Page** – all the columns in the print area will be scaled down to fit one page, however, the rows can carry on into other pages.

- **Fit All Rows into One Page** – all rows in the print area will be scaled to fit one page, however, the columns can carry on into other pages.

5. I find the **Fit All Columns on One Page** scaling option to be the most appropriate for most spreadsheet documents. This lets you see all data pertaining to a single row on one page.

6. Always view your document in the preview pane to ensure you're happy with the layout before printing it. This would save you a tonne of ink and paper. There are page numbers at the bottom of the screen that enables you to scroll through the pages to see what will be printed.

7. Click on **Print** to print the document.

12 SECURING YOUR WORKBOOK

Excel enables you to protect your workbook with a password to prevent others from editing your data, deleting worksheets, or renaming worksheets in the workbook.

Note: Before you protect your workbook with a password, ensure that you've got the password written down and stored in a safe place where it can be retrieved if necessary. Without a password cracking tool, it is impossible to gain access to an Excel file that has been password-protected if the password has been forgotten.

How to set a password for your Excel workbook:

1. Click on **File** > **Save As** (or press **F12**).
2. Click on the **More options** link (which is directly under the file type box). This will launch the **Save As** window.

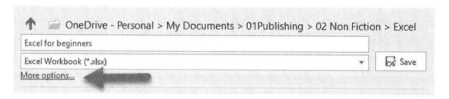

3. On the **Save As** window, click on the **Tools** drop-down list and select **General Options** from the menu.

   A dialogue box will be displayed that enables you to set a password required to open the workbook and a password required to modify the workbook.

4. Enter a password in the **Password to open** box, and then click OK.
5. Re-enter the password in the **Confirm Password** box, and then click OK.
6. Click on **Save**, and then select **Yes** If you wish to replace the existing file.

Set a password to modify an Excel file:

1. Click on **File** > **Save As** (or press **F12**).
2. Click on the **More options...** link. This will launch the **Save As** window.
3. In the **Save As** window, click on the **Tools** drop-down and select **General Options** from the menu. A dialogue box will be displayed that enables you to set a password required to open the workbook and the password required to modify the workbook.
4. Enter a password in the **Password to modify** box, and then click OK.
5. Confirm the password in the next dialogue box and then click OK.
6. Click **Save**, and then select **Yes** If you wish to replace the existing file.

Set different passwords to open and modify an Excel file:

1. Select **File** > **Save As** (or press **F12**).
2. Click on **More options...**
3. In the **Save As** window, click on the **Tools** drop-down list, and then select **General Options**.
4. Enter different passwords in the **Password to modify** and **Password to open** boxes, and then click OK.
5. The **Confirm Password** box will be displayed twice, enabling you to re-enter both passwords to confirm them. Re-enter both passwords and click OK each time.

Click **Save**, and then select **Yes** If you wish to replace the existing file.

86

ABOUT THE AUTHOR

Nathan George is a Computer Science graduate and worked for several years as an analyst/programmer and web developer in the IT services industry before entering the dotcom world as a digital entrepreneur. One of his main interests is using computers to automate tasks and increase productivity. As an author, he has written several fiction and non-fiction books.

OTHER BOOKS BY AUTHOR

WordPress For Beginners
A Visual Guide To Building Your WordPress Site + 22 Top WordPress Plugins

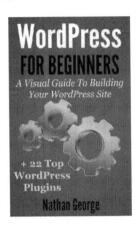

Available at Amazon:
https://www.amazon.com/dp/B06XCMRLC6

Convert Your Text To Audio
Boost Your Reading Capacity And Speed Using Free Tools Like Audacity

Available at Amazon:
https://www.amazon.com/dp/B01EBLTZCC

Made in the USA
Lexington, KY
31 October 2017